*poe*HEART*ic*

(Rhythms of Love…)

Adebayo Kolawole Samuel

*poe*HEART*ic*

(Rhythms of Love...)

Adebayo Kolawole Samuel

WORDS
RHYMES &
RHYTHM

Printed and Published in Nigeria by:
Words Rhymes & Rhythm Limited
Suite C309, Global Plaza Plot 366, Obafemi
Awolowo Way, Jabi District, Abuja, Nigeria.
08169027757, 08060109295
www.wrr.ng

CONTENTS

DEDICATION

To hearts and the music they play...

PRAISE FOR *POEHEARTIC*

"Kolawole's offering would deflate and inflate you. It would make you sing and mutter the letters of silence. This powerful collection is the first stroke in a promising swim. This voice does not want to drown. This voice wouldn't. Powerful collection!"

— Adedayo Adeyemo Agarau,
Author of *For Boys Who Went*

"There is an instigating pressure that brings the words into life, which is a sheer testament to the magic love holds in our eyes, in a way. Adebayo defined healing and home in a single word, which the world needs to breathe again."

— Mesioye Johnson; Award winning poet, Co-author of *Rainbows And Fireflies*

"Love without a voice is lifeless, so is a life without love worthless. Kolawole's heart-rending, and seething poems connect with the divine state of the heart. A wildfire ignited softly. Many voices muffled into lines of thought. This poet's heart is of gold. Glowing!

— Wale Ayinla, Editor, Critic, and author of *White Roses* and *The Other Side of Other Rooms*

FOREWORD

Love is a journey. And to undertake such experience within the radius of the pen is a serious business of a patient pilot of poetics. And yet again, to write about love, is documenting the soul— and more often, a searchlight for revival. Here, is Adebayo in whom I am well pleased.

Adebayo is undoubtedly a serious mind; a confident custodian of love. He departs with the fire of "revival" and revival here is very symbolic. Life. That love is an effort to live from the haunts in "'espresso". That love is a "'song of songs" to bring about "rhythms" to the hurts of "sad songs". That love is breath to every deadness. There is a pilgrimage intent in "wash me"— and laying bare. A total surrender to love. The "longing" in "me" is converting.

To say love is cleansing, is valid.

Without doubt, Adebayo's poeHEARTic is a gripping artistic evidence. It makes the heart tick—it makes a thick heart break into an indescribable softness. Something dotingly cozy. The reader's sense of appreciation is quickly awoken. At first, to a radiation of aesthetic trappings of fine poetics, then ingenuity and at the same time a resounding call to love and love genuinely.

One other beautiful thing about this collection is that the poet does not fail to expose the polarity existence in love; the ills and heals, the heartbreak and heart-mending, the heat and cold, the cut and court— as a way of saying love is beautiful— as a way of saying love is strictly for mature minds, not for babes or cowards who misunderstand "falling" in love as a parade of ridicule.

Adebayo's sight is plain. He sees respect, equality and oneness as able companions for love to be love, something evidently missing in the love expressed nowadays. Adebayo shines a new light on love; that love is being beautifully and uniquely senseless. He keeps for posterity epistles of love— to a son, to a daughter, to a husband, to a wife, to the young and old — to serve as stand-by buoys as one drowns in the waters of love.

The exploration of love in this collection is bright and brilliant— an act of pruning and creating a renewed platform to approach love and sensuality and the consciousness exuded in the use of language is equally simple and profound, a safe channel to tread to touch love that is love.

Of a note in poeHEARTic, the woman, as a symbol of love, is roundly glorified. O Woman! I hail o.

Who says love is not capable of resurrection? Adebayo's poeHEARTic IS a resounding answer!

— Ayoola Goodness
Author of Meditations
Ogun, Nigeria

love is a rhythm of the heart
masked sometimes in hues of hurts
and feelings folded on faces buried in gloom,
revealed when we welcome the choral notes
playing on the keyboard of our hearts;
on the keyboard of our hearts...

REVIVAL
(for that woman who is fire…)

i was dead,
buried in the cold dark grave
of loneliness and feelings that
make a heart lost in the embrace of gloom.
life sang me an elegy of broken things,
shattered love, shriveled smiles, languid laughs
by the urn of that man who drank love as a river
into his belly of a thousand fathoms— me.
and i told myself that i wouldn't yield my heart no
more
to gods of desires and goddesses of love,
of rising heartbeats
of sweaty palms
of mutterings and babblings
of the songs a man sings to a woman
of the words he writes on frail silent nights
and the promises he makes on glad new morns.
i walked into a city of revival
and i found healing in the wings of a fair lady.
lips are wings. fingers are wings. smiles are wings.
thighs are wings. faces are wings. bodies are wings.
i drank of elixirs of resurrection and immortality
(i believe these elixirs are true);
like a phoenix, Cupid is risen from grey ashes.
i pray this revival isn't a fluke.
to die twice is hard for a man.

you are my revival. be true.
let a man not die again.

ESPRESSO

i sipped my coffee
and you came back to me
like a phoenix rising from ruins
and i tried to spew you out of my mouth
but you are espresso;
you leave your shadow in a place
and it comes alive in the light of my coffee.
and i sip more and more
and my belly sings of forgotten things;
of feelings i flung far from freedom of expression.
i wish i never smelled your hair
and your body and your breath.
now my coffee haunts me.

SAD SONGS
(i will not be mad again...)

you broke me into two
and left me in the ICU
of hearts that bleed
for love that never finds them
and i am in my clothes
of oxygen mask and blue linen
of feelings that crept into my heart
when i let down my guard;
you are the enemy who sows tares
when a farmer sleeps at night;
(but you are not an enemy;
my heart bled love for you)
what am i even saying?
now i'm mad— confusion.
am i the enemy of myself?
i who left my head
in hot springs of emotions
for a bath that batted my brain
into flurry blurry drains
of sadness and tears.
i am telling you,
other patients in our ICU,
these are the last teardrops
i will let loose from my eyes of wells
tomorrow is another day;
i will not be mad again

and springs will fail to bathe me with bats.
yesterday is gone.
today, i am crying;
tomorrow is another day
i will not be mad again...

WASH ME

sky,
rain your tears
on me.
cry waters of heaven
on my body of many journeys
into places like the falls of Victoria
and the dry lands of New Zealand with zeal,
and wash my flesh
away from memories that haunt the soul,
hunting for feelings that tear the heart into two

feelings of a lady i should forget,
touches i should forget,
smiles i should forget,
hairs i should forget,
lips i should forget...
open the floodgates of heaven,
let it rain.
let her be washed
into earth.

but here is the curse;
when a seed falls into the soil,
it grows into children of a thousand names;
like yesterday,
how the rains washed my flesh
and today feelings are growing in the earth

in the womb of my soul...
in the womb of my soul...

ME

drink me
into your lungs
like how a drunk longs
for a bottle of iced whiskey.
he reaches out for his cup
and stretches for his bottle
buried in the igloo of a fridge
and he pours and pours and pores
on the foaming liquor and pours again
and he sips and sips again then pauses and gulps
and he is raptured into a place of trees looking as
men.
drink me like that!
let me numb your senses
and make you smile for a cough
and make you cackle 'cos i told you
i muffle my breaths when i greet the khazi.
drink me poco a poco.
smell my cologne.
watch my strides.
touch my face.
ah! lips...

yes,
walk on my lips
with your two legs of lips
and stand firm thereon to stay.

then fall into my arms,
like a drunk falling into the arms of wine,
and see an even rise out a mooned morn
and see yourself ride an Ostrich with me into Mars.

i am a fine blend
of oats of charm
and barleys of panache.
pour me.
drink me.
let me serenade you
into a senseless haven!

LOVE IS A SILENCE OF WORDS
(of the words we speak without moving our lips...)

i lie here
thinking about
the way a star gently walks
into a sky knighted in darkness— night—
and you come into my mind;
how you sauntered
into my heart
like a star
into a sky.

you are an ode
that rises softly
but hits the heart
like a mighty running wind,
and i am broken, and i am shattered.

there are pieces of me
crawling inside you
here and there
like how air
is here and there.
you are my place
of brokenness
and silence.
and silence
can be louder

than a million words.
i am in that place
where lips don't move
but words are spoken.

you will hear them in the wind
you will feel them through a touch.
you will taste them through tongues and lips.

i have broken into you
the way you sauntered into me
as a star struts into a sky knighted into night.
and i am in that place of silence;
lips are not walking,
words are falling.

i am stroking
your hair of dark sheen
and you can hear the words
that a touch gently-loudly speaks.
it is saying them now:
i love you.

it will speak them again tomorrow:
i love you.

TWINKLE

two winking little stars
gliding in the air that blows
on a night when two legs walk
to that tall tree beside riverbank.

they are smiling at each other
like the way faces owned by four legs
that have walked to a tree beside a bank
       a r e   s m i l i n g.

twinkle is the story
of my mom and dad.
he took her to a coconut tree
by the bank of the river in their village

and he said:
"look at those two stars,
i have named them after us.
and we will always smile like them."

and there he planted the seed of a kiss
in the earth of her forehead
and it grew a fire within her.

that fire burned me out— birth.
i'm the child of the first night of betrothal.

i'm the son of the first fire my father kindled
in the blank belly of a young beautiful lass—
mother.

they are still twinkling.
they are smiling, and i am here learning
how to twinkle to that woman
that would walk with me
to see stars by a shore:

two winking little stars
gliding in the air that blows
on a night when four legs shall
walk to a shore in a port of Harcourt.

FALLING...

i am Jericho wall.
but you are breaking
       i
       n
       t
       o
      my
   h   t
    e r
     a

with a Jewish shout,
like the way a wave rolls itself
around a sinking ship on raging seas—
the voice of waters and thunder and lightning.

you are the crumbling
of a wall long built.
and i am falling by
(into) your mighty
shout— love.

LONGINGS I
(of the fire that burns espoused beings...)

The depth
of your kiss
is like fire in my mouth.
It burns me into ashes of longings.

Here I am;
dead—
buried in
that place
where my lips
have burrowed—
inside your mouth.

LONGINGS II
(of the cold a traveling husband begins...)

Here I am
with my lips trembling
on a sunny day as this.

It is you
freezing me from within.
I am cold but I am sweating.

Passersby think I am mad
for wearing a sweater
in this hell of a sun.

But I know the cold
I am dealing with.
And I love this heat.
It's my comfort-place.

Your absence is ice.
Your presence is fire.
Come quickly. I want to burn
like I did the first night of our espousal.

RHYTHMS...

(tonight, I beg wordy gods for the metaphors
 that paint plain pictures on hearted canvasses...)

Your name is the song
that nightly winds sing
into the ears of sleeping souls.

Your face is the clouds
that wear dark masks:
rainy blessings are here.

You are the palm tree
behind my grandfather's hut;
tall, strong, and prettily fruity.

You are the words
that gods cannot find;
like air, they feel your weight
(air is weighty— it's life's home);

but like dumb mouths,
they watch in awe.

WHEN A DEAD BOY RISES AGAIN…

dreams:
i once loved a lady
who promised we'd marry
and make beautiful black babies.

she was a ray
slitting through
my heart like a knife
on burial cow's neck.

on foggy beds of dreams,
i kiss my pretty bride.
i wear me a golden ring
and ring her finger in diamond.

i made beautiful black babies
with that lady i married
in lofty dreams.

it's the way i grew up,
dreaming of that girl
who lived next flat.
i never told her…

i'm grown up now.
i know high school music(als)

was (were) sung into my eyes of a boy.
i was dreaming myself into a nowhere of stars

but there's another girl next flat now
and stars were truly gone
until bloody last night
when that boy in me
arose again.

i know this kind of dream and
i am smiling and asking me:
shall i kill this boy
or let him loose?

JOURNEYING THROUGH HURTS

Some mornings,
I wake up on
the wings of poetry.

4a.m.
I am thinking words
and the things they do
to a woman's ears on dark nights.

The way
they walk
down that lane
into her white heart

like how a ball
walks in Brownian motion
at White Hart Lane— Tottenham.

5a.m.
It is you.
It is you who
brings myriads of words
into my memory of singing nights.

Of the words
I sang down that hall
into your white heart.

Of the way I held your hands
like how a rain holds coldness.
Of how you laughed like a new born babe
when I tickled you into a heaven of laughters.

Of how we were
lying down next to each other
staring into the sky like a country of grasses
watching the cinema that plays in full moons.

Of the things we did
(I will not reveal secrets),
of how you left me on a lonely night
of the cold that bites at a man's flesh
and the one that rouses a man on
new mornings of aloneness
and brokenness.

6a.m.
I'll make coffee.
I'll kill this cold.
You're gone. I'll live.

7a.m.
I am walking out my door.
I am smelling the air of a Friday.
I am smiling. I am breathing. I am living.

HOW I THINK I WILL FALL IN LOVE

i have seen big breasts
become flaggy
like a loaf left overnight in water.
i have seen aged mouths without teeth
& some with scattered sets
like walls full of cracks,
like baskets decorated with holes.

last month i visited my grandma
& she wasn't the voluptuous figure
in her photobook anymore,
& my mind wandered into a wonder:
what was grandpa still loving about her?
i asked myself a question of sincerity:
what would their coitus be?
two tired bodies entering into each other,
one reclining fraily upon another weak bone...

i know wrinkles
are a future for all flesh
to walk into.
so when i think about love,
i think about the end.

i know the mind still works at old age.
i know an octogenarian can be a sage.
i know wisdom in an old body can be center of a
stage.
i know ideas are the torches that shine in darkness.

so, what then is a body
without a sound mind?
it is but a painted coffin,
a night without a moon,
an empty drum,
a clanging cymbal,
mascara of nothingness!

i know beautiful bodies
are havens of delights,
but a beautiful body
with a mind as parched as a wilderness
is the pathway into brokenness.

so, this is how i think i will fall in love:
the mind first,
then the body
then the mammary,
then the ham.

yes,
that is how i will fall in love.

SONG OF SONGS

Come my love,
my lips have fallowed
and the nutrients are bold.

Plant yours upon mine
and let us grow a thing
that wrecks the body
into a silence of silences.

Come my love,
let us sing songs
that only lips can hear.

Strum your way into my heart
with words that rapture my pores
into a place of senseless sense.

Come my love,
let us begin our song of songs
and sing until all we hear
is silence;

a silence
that turns our ears
into "feelingless" things.

YOU

You walk upon
the marbled floor of my soul
     like stars upon clouds,
      l
      i
      n
      e
      d
on the endless rope of nightly skies.

You are the movement
         on the land of my heart
making pathways through verdure
of dark feelings that rise from past voyages
into cities where love is the song on every lip.

MY SINGLE HOPE

I cannot be a poet before you
for the song that your name sings
is too strong for my pen to bear.

I cannot be a man of words to you
for to correctly describe you
is to be locked away in dark alleys
in a vain attempt to describe a shadow.

Is it wearing a green or blue shirt?
Is it crying or smiling?

I cannot be a singer either!
For what song shall I render?
You already are an orchestra of
beautifully mellifluous sounds

bound together by a harmonious chord
of love, laughter, and joy.

But I cannot forever say I cannot;
for how shall I make you know
the thrummings of my heart
if I do not write?

How shall you listen to my song
if I do not sing?

Therefore, I shall write the few words
which my frail hands find
on the soft paper of your soul.

I shall also sing the few notes
which my fragile vocal cords can carry
to the sweet ears of your heart.

And this only;
this only is my single hope:
"Perhaps...
She might even tell me I can.
Perhaps..."

I WROTE MY SON A POEM
(loving a girl...)

son,
there are days you'll find yourself
lost in the country of a girl,
and she'll be beautiful
and send you into a town
where stars are shining night and day;
and you will be afraid that you are losing it,
that your logic is failing you,
that your heart is running into madness.
do not be afraid;
love is a city
where we lose ourselves in another
(and we only find ourselves
when we are lost).
love her;
you will be glad you did.

yours,
father.

I WROTE MY DAUGHTER A POEM
(learning to wait for love...)

daughter,
when you wake in the morning,
learn to lift your two hands into the air
and breathe in the freshness of a new day.
learn to say to yourself
that you will not fall into the hole i fell into,
that you will not allow yourself enter into a man
who does not know how to love a woman,
that you will not allow a man whose heart
is shrouded in dark mists of misogyny
to sweep you off your feet and carry you
into the bedroom at the other side
(love is another side of life
and we are all journeying there)
tell him you are not ready to go
if he will not learn to pluck the stars in your eyes
with love in his two eyes
and peace in his two hands;
tell him you will not bend
in his wind of cacophonies,
that your mother told you about him
before her body became one with dust,
that you will wait there learning to breathe,
learning to live with strength in your heart
until the man who crawls into your sleep

and whose dream you are
comes searching for you
with the kind of charm
that the morning rises with.

yours,
mother.

HOW TO LOVE A WOMAN

Walk into that city
that lives in her heart
and leave yourself inside it
like the sun left on the sky.

Sometimes, you will not like the city
for the noise that bleeds inside it—
the voices of a thousand things;
child and you, this and that…

And you will turn your ears away
from scattered notes
of songs that spring from chaos
and noise, and voices, and words.

But learn
that a woman is music
that scatters into formation.
You will not like these tones
in the beginning of their lives

but your ears will leap,
like a goat enraptured
by the scent of verdure,
by the tunes that scattered tones
become in the end.

Live and leave yourself
in this city.
Follow the way of notes and tones
and find the tune that a woman is:
sweet music; pleasant and sonorous.

And you will find yourself
singing out loud the music
that your woman is,
and leaving
yourself
inside
her.

HOW TO LOVE A MAN

i am a man
and my fingers wobble
like the feet of an old man
nearing the gate of his grave
because to write
of the way to love a man
is like finding the air that enters
into fire and makes it burn into red.

i can't write
of the way i feel
when a woman's hands
touches the skin of my heart

but i know that
i like to breathe her
into my nostrils till i fill
my belly with sweetness.
i'll tell you this:
fold yourself neatly
into the air that walks
with the rise of a new day

and enter into
the nostrils of a man.
enter therein with the scent
of words that turn a man into hardness:

"You're my husband,
my love, king and friend."
enter therein as an AK-47
ready to battle by his side

the demons that scorn
a man's mornings into mournings,
and walk therein with the legs of things
that make a man's belly sing sweet songs

of satisfaction
and the sensation
that comes from eatables.
so, enter with these things

and settle perfectly
in his heart like dust upon plates.
& you will see that a man is a baby.
& you will see that he will suck
the sweet breasts of your scent
and drink into his belly
the sweetness that your body is.

MELODIES OF A HUSBAND

Have you seen my wife?
She is like the dance of grasses
To the music of harmattan winds—
Swift. Soft. Gentle. Coy. Lovely. Beauty.

Have you seen her hair?
They are as dark as the darkness
Of a starless night— Black. Black. Black.

Have you seen her smile?
It's the sun that shines after rainfall.
It will rise softly out of cloudiness
And fill the heart of the earth with warmth?

Who are you O anger
Before the smile of my wife?
Thou shall melt as wax before flames
And perish as Egyptian Chariots in a Sea of Red.

My wife is my music
And the muse of new mornings.
She is the glory of sunset
And the clothing of a bright moon.

I will sing you,
Even as I sing now,

And dance to you
Even as I dance now.

I will sleep inside you
And pluck words
From the beauty
That you are.

HEARTBREAK

I am walking
Like a shadow
In dark places.

Do you see
Shadow in
The dark?

You will not see me.
But I am here
Whimpering

Like the coldness
Of a lone night.
Alone, I cry

My eyes
Into a Red Sea
Of tears that drown

Chariots that run riot
On that way that runs
Through the valleys in my heart.

I am shadow
Walking through

The valley of a pool of tears.

There is no light.
You are gone.
No light...

SONGS OF FIREFLIES

i write of songs that fireflies sing.
i hear them.
They sing

the song a mother
sings into her child's ears.
a song of winds and wings
of birds that fly, and those that walk

of hills and valleys
of meadows and alleys
of caves and mountains
of suns and stars and moons
and rivers, and streams and oceans

and the little things we let by
and those we forget to say

like "i love you"
like "i miss you"
like "i am sorry"

this poem is singing.
are you listening?

JON SNOW
(you know nothing...)

i said i love you
and you bent your ears away
like how a leaf shakes her behind
in winds that dance upon nightly clouds.

you are Jon.
you know nothing.
i am that fire that melts wax
into a procession of marching waters.

i will burn your heart
into ashes of desires.
i will walk you into a rapture,
into heavens of smiles and cacophonies.

i am Ygritte;
and like Jon Snow,
you know nothing…
you know nothing...

SOURSOP

I ate a soursop today
after almost ten years of breakup with it.
It tasted heavenly; soothing my throat,
and serenading my belly with its cold allure.

Its taste reminded me of Àsàkè,
the daughter of the palm wine tapper;
of Àbèké, the daughter of the Akara seller;
and Àdùké, the daughter of Balógun (warlord).

The 'sop tasted like
what my tongue felt
when I and Àsàkè did all we did
under that mango tree in the sight of dusky airs.

Things which my small mouth
must never speak, and my blue pen
must never storify on the papers of time.

The white flesh of the 'sop
was like Àbèké's lips; soft and lush.
I tore into it with a passion indefinable;
I must feel her lips again inside this 'sop.

The kisses of Àdùké
were homed in the 'sop.
As always, they tasted like paradise;

Mentos carefully mixed with Milkose!

What I ate today
was not just a fruit;
in it was a resurrection of dead flames,
and a reinvigoration of buried memories.

I must revive Àsàké!
I must awaken Àbèké!
I must resurrect Àdùké!
Morrow must be another feast on 'sop!

ÀWÈRÓ MI (MY ÀWÈRÓ)

Àwèrò mi,
that year, you gave me your heart
and I gave you mine.
It was an exchange; heart for heart;
soul for soul.

The day was February 13,
a day before the world marked its own love.
It had to be that day.
For, our own love would help light lanterns
in hearts devoid of love's lucid light.

It was underneath that palm tree,
beside the crystal clear stream that
swims into the River Awéléwà (River of beauties),
that we first took our oaths.

The Sun had intensely kissed green leaves
and they smiled at the delight of his lips;
warm, luscious, lively, fizzy;
tender and soft like freshly baked bread.

It was from him that I learnt the way around your
lips;
It was he who taught me how to navigate the crooks
and the bends.
He showed me a fire that burns

but never destroys.

Àwèrò,
Remember how we burnt together?
How we swam desirously in the lake of fire
produced by our intense passion?

It was the gentle current of affection
keeping us afloat on Love's lake of fire.

It was upon the black earth on which that palm tree
built its castle
that we first saw the color of each other's heart.
Mine was red and yours white.
They were the colors that would come with the day
that followed the day our exchange took place.

My red heart is firmly fitted
in the white bosom behind your immaculate breasts
and yours is in the red home behind
this sturdy chest of mine.

Àwèrò mi,
I write this to put you in remembrance
that we must never come apart.
For we both bore each other's soul
while the Sun gently serenaded green leaves.

Àwèrò mi,

we must never come apart.
For, our hearts are intertwined.
Your beat is my beat.
My beat is your beat.

Àwèrò mi,
I know 30 years have breezed past us now
and we have enjoyed such heavenly bliss.
But, a little reminder would do no harm.

Happy anniversary to us Àwèrò!
I, Dáúdù òré aláso (friend of the cloth-maker),
love you with all my heart!

LOVE

is the name of little shiny stars
singing over a gathering of clouds
by twilight,
hitting mellow notes
on the piano of a woman's body;
they are singing in the mouth of a man
who is lost in the country of a woman's face;
he is going here and there
finding home in her body.
love is the song a woman becomes
for a man to play
and sing
and listen to.
this doesn't make sense!
a bearded man is smiling
like a baby dreaming of candy floss
and a full breasted woman is hugging a teddy;
she names it after him
and kisses it (him) before night dies.
love is a city where senses are numbed.
but sometimes, one must try to revive medulla
for love may swallow you into her belly
and deliver you into hell
if medulla is fully dead.
but then too,
love is a city where revival is hard.
revival is hard...

let us pray for revival.
let fire fall down from heaven...

LET LOVE FLY

music is an archipelago
of islands of melodies
strung upon notes
soaked in waters
of harmony;
baritones
tritones
sopranos
and tenors
and altos altering
the configuration of hearts...
music is the force that calms
a sea raging with feelings of hatred
and brokenness of unspeakable levels.

love is music.
hearts are seas.
there is healing in the wings of love,
ointments and balms from countries
like Cyprus and Lebanon, where winds
whistle tunes of life, and light, and hope,
soothing skins, returning strength to frail bones.

now play the music,
and let love fly
high into the sky.

we
are all
getting
healed...

I IN YOU, YOU IN ME

(a poem of oneness in love...)

girl,
my mind is not a blank paper
for you to write yourself on.
i have waded within high waters and prevailed.
i have walked through fire unscathed.
do you know the flames
that come from smoked wood?
maybe; i don't know the places you've been too.
but don't come thinking you can turn me
into one man you watched in Bollywood movies.
i am not a weasel who whistles tunes of winds every
time,
playing hide and seek with emotions.
there are memories i bear in my body
you may not understand.
there are names i house in my head
you may not know how to call.
so, let the two become one.
accept me as i accept you.

love is not a hurricane
that imposes itself
on houses,
turning them
into piles of s-a-d-n-e-s-s.
love is a leaf that kisses a bar soap.
when a leaf lives long with soap,

soap becomes leaf,
leaf becomes soap...

we will be one
if we learn to
bury our past in our present;
telling ourselves everybody isn't the same,
telling ourselves he will not cheat,
telling ourselves she will not defile our sheets
after we get married under the sun.

girl,
i will be him
if you give me time.
time sometimes erases the past.
my mind can become blank again
if you swallow me up in the body of time

one day,
you will become
the blankness of my heart.
it may be 50 years or 40 or 20
or even less

but i know one day,
we will say:
"i in you & you in me;
the leaf and the soap have become one!"
i love you...

I AM A POEM IN YOUR HEART
(you are a poem in my heart...)

woman,
i am a poem in your heart
and there is nothing you
can do about me.

i have built a home of words
in the corridors of your womb.
so the first seed my phallus shall spew
(when on that night when time shall stand still
for the consummation of love in songs of moans)
shall be at home inside your womb.

the boy
(he will be a boy)
will know that i once came there
riding on the sleigh of words
before i came again in him.

i am a poem in your womb.
i am the first child you carried
before the coming in of our seed.
shall a woman run away from the child
singing words in her womb?

it is hard to run away from one's heart.
tell your father that you can't
walk the aisle with that bloody muppet

who came with a convoy of cars & puppets
opening his door for him.

you cannot allow your father
to turn your womb into ruins.
tell him you have given your heart to another,

tell him there's a man inside your womb
in the body of a poem,
telling you of the future,

of your boy child who will be a poet,
of sundowns and sunups,
of lips kissing in meadows,
of love that never wanes,
of hearts devoid of stains...

and if he will not listen,
remember i am a poem in your heart
and you are a poem in my heart,
then follow down that path
to the tavern where we met,
let us run into the future we have written.

we will come back to him.
what can the past do
when the future comes visiting?

i love you...

EVE

i played my fingers
on the piano of a body
and i felt my heart hear him— God:

that a bone can become flesh,
that a flesh can be smoother than glass panes,
that eyes can house the sun,
that lips can be oceans of comfort,
that beauty can be named after a body.

eve...

i christened the body woman
i named the lips love
i called the eyes eve.

i, high on her eyes of wines, smiled
and swore an oath with time;
that the wind will whisk her every night into heaven
in the poetry of my fingers,
writing a ballad of love on her heart.

i, drunk with beers of barleys in bodies, blushed
for her smile and her dark eyeballs
for her hair, and the dark sheen,
for her hips, and the curved roads,

for her hands, and the silent touches
that turn a man into a movie of goats and verdure.

eve...

come.
bone of my body.
flesh of my bones.
cleave unto me. let us be one.

eve...

GLOSSARY

- Àsàké, Àbèké, Àdùké, Àwèrò, and Awéléwà are all Yoruba names.

ABOUT THE AUTHOR

Adebayo Kolawole Samuel is a budding Nigerian poet based in Akure, the capital city of Ondo State in South-Western Nigeria.

He is regarded one of the most talented young, contemporary African poets and his writings, which he says are based on the conviction that "words are one of the world's greatest assets," have enjoyed wide readership, especially on social media platforms.

Adebayo is the winner of the Brigitte Poirson Poetry Contest (April, 2017). His writings have been published on several reputable platforms.

He studied Agricultural Extension and Communication Technology at the Federal University of Technology, Akure, Ondo State.

www.ingramcontent.com/pod-product-compliance
Lightning Source LLC
Chambersburg PA
CBHW032053040426
42449CB00007B/1097